PATRIOTIC SYMBOLS

The White House

Nancy Harris

Heinemann Library
Chicago, Illinois

Customer Service **888-454-2279**

Visit our Web site at **www.heinemannlibrary.com**

Photo research by Tracy Cummins
Designed by Kimberly R. Miracle
Maps by Mapping Specialists, Ltd.
Printed and bound in China by South China Printing Company

10 09 08 07
10 9 8 7 6 5 4 3 2 1

10 Digit ISBN: 1-4034-9383-9 (hc)   1-4034-9390-1 (pb)

Library of Congress Cataloging-in-Publication Data
Harris, Nancy, 1956-
  The White House / Nancy Harris.
    p. cm. -- (Patriotic symbols)
  Includes bibliographical references and index.
  ISBN 978-1-4034-9383-5 (hc) -- ISBN 978-1-4034-9390-3 (pb) 1. White House (Washington, D.C.)--Juvenile literature. 2. Washington (D.C.)--Buildings, structures, etc.--Juvenile literature. 3. Signs and symbols--United States--Juvenile literature. I. Title.
  F204.W5H384 2007
  975.3--dc22
                                          2006039379

Acknowledgements
The author and publisher are grateful to the following for permission to reproduce copyright material: ©Alamy **p. 6** (Steve Allen); ©AP Photo **pp. 18** (Karin Cooper), 19 (Roberto Borea), 23 (Koji Sasahara); ©Corbis **pp. 5** (flag, Royalty Free), 9 (Bettmann), 11 (Reuters/Larry Downing), 13 (Bettmann), 14 (Wally McNamee), 17, 21 (Wally McNamee), 23 (Wally McNamee); ©Getty Images **pp. 5** (eagle, Don Farrall), 8 (Mitchell Funk), 10 (AFP), 12 (Rex Banner), 16 (Alex Wong), 20 (AFP), 23 (Alex Wong); ©The Granger Collection **p. 15** (Rue des Archives); ©istockphoto **p. 5** (Liberty Bell, drbueller); ©Shutterstock **pp. 4** (Uli), **5** (Statue of Liberty, Ilja Mašík).

Cover image reproduced with permission of ©Shutterstock (Uli). Back cover image reproduced with permission of ©Alamy (Steve Allen).

Every effort has been made to contact copyright holders of any material reproduces in this book.
Any omissions will be rectified in subsequent printings if notice is given to the publisher.

Contents

What Is a Symbol?

The White House is a symbol.
A symbol is a type of sign.

A symbol shows you something.

The White House

The White House is a special symbol.

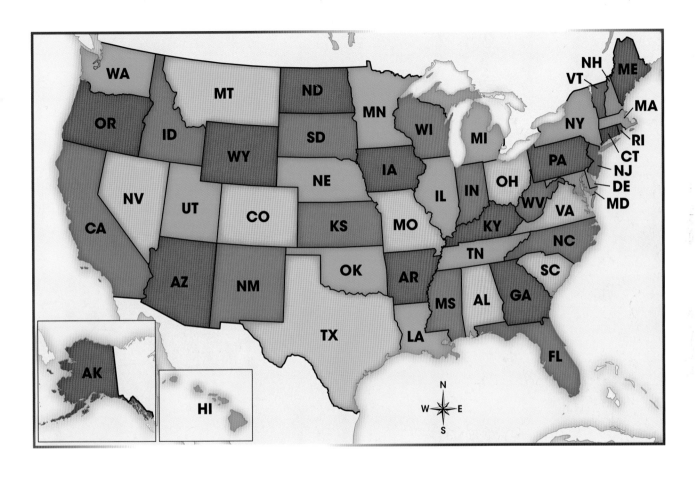

It is a symbol of the United States of America.
The United States of America is a country.

The White House is a patriotic symbol.

It shows the beliefs of the country. It shows
how people in the country work together.

The President

The president lives in the White House.

First Family

The president's family lives there, too.

The president is the leader of the country.
The president leads the United States.

The White House is a symbol of leadership.

The Oval Office

Oval Office

The Oval Office is in the White House.

The president works in the Oval Office.

The Oval Office is a symbol of the president.

The Cabinet Room

Cabinet Room

The Cabinet Room is in the White House. The president works with people there to lead the country.

The White House is a symbol of working with others to lead the country.

Visitors

People are welcome to visit the White House.

The White House is a symbol of the American people. It belongs to all the people in the country.

What It Tells You

The White House tells you where and how the president works.

The president works with people to lead
the country.

White House Facts

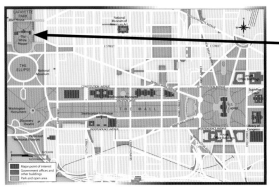

★ The White House is in Washington, D.C.

★ The White House is more than 200 years old.

Timeline

1700   1750   1792   1800

✪ The White House was first built in 1792. It was finished in 1800.

Picture Glossary

 **Cabinet Room** the room where the president meets with important people

 **country** an area of land that is ruled by the same leader

 **Oval Office** the room where the president works

 **patriotic** believing in your country

Index

Note to Parents and Teachers

The study of patriotic symbols introduces young readers to our country's government and history. Books in this series begin by defining a symbol before focusing on the history and significance of a specific patriotic symbol. Use the timeline and facts section on page 22 to introduce readers to these non-fiction features.

The text has been carefully chosen with the advice of a literacy expert to enable beginning readers success while reading independently or with moderate support. An expert in the field of early childhood social studies curriculum was consulted to provide interesting and appropriate content.

You can support children's nonfiction literacy skills by helping students use the table of contents, headings, picture glossary, and index.